HOW THINGS ARE ON THURSDAY

T0159763

ROS BARBER

How Things Are on Thursday

Anvil Press Poetry

Published in 2004
by Anvil Press Poetry Ltd
Neptune House 70 Royal Hill London SE10 8RF
www.anvilpresspoetry.com

Copyright © Ros Barber 2004

This book is published with financial assistance
from Arts Council England

Designed and set in Monotype Bulmer by Anvil
Printed at Alden Press Limited
Oxford and Northampton

ISBN 0 85646 374 4

For my mother

Acknowledgements

Acknowledgements are due to the editors of the following
publications in which some of these poems first appeared:
*Anvil New Poets 3, Equinox, Leviathan Quarterly, MsLexia,
The North, Orbis, Poetry Review, Rattapallax* (USA), *Stand,
Tabla New Verse 2000*, and *What Will We Do When We Get
There?*

'Waiting for Scott' was highly commended in the National
Poetry Competition 1987; 'Well' was commended in the
same competition in 1997; both appeared in the pamphlet
of winning poems.

'Embassy Court' was written for the Arts Council's
ArchiTEXTs project. 'Fecundity' was written for *Impressions
of Wealden*. 'Who Forgets' was commissioned by Company
Gavin Robertson to accompany the show *I Am Who Am I?*
'Soup' was one of a sequence of poems commissioned by
Sustrans and Kent County Council for the Chalk & Channel
Way, and 'BN1' was commissioned by Project Poetry.

Lastly, thanks are due to Catherine Smith, and to Paul,
for being there when it mattered.

Contents

How Things Are on Thursday

Liberation

The weather person shapes a bulletin
around this week in nineteen fifty-one;
then depth of snow off-piste in Val d'Isère,
the unusually heavy rain for the time of year
in northern Mexico. Not a thing about the English
weather, now. Not a single place she'll likely go.

In the other room, her children snap and spark
like static shocks, trickle-charged through years
of a marriage that chafed their parents' artificial
hides. Little capacitors. She feels from them
volts of their father not properly earthed,
not even by their trailing *love-me* wires.

Once, she thought she lived in fifty-one.
Accepted, like a pelt, her husband's coat,
slippered a carpet soured with baby piss
as neglected potatoes galloped their way to soup.
At night, unpegging washing from the line,
damp with dew, it was hard to go back in.

That was old-fashioned dying. This is new:
the late night bottle of budget red, alone.
Drunken keyboard chats with strangers who
haven't the foggiest who they're typing to.
At least she gets to pass out when she wants.
At least she gets to stay in her outside shoes.

Lafayette Super Eight

I

The flickering stills of seventy-one. The yellow slant
of West Coast sunlight or the mellowing of celluloid
makes us foreigners in our own childhoods.

The hill-perched house and ourselves shrunk by the decades;
our unseen futures—now our histories—etched faintly over
our faces like ghosts hoaxed onto copper-plates.

Our voices too distant to carry to screen; the medium's
silence complete with the transfer to video. I miss
the projector's clack. We are slightly out of tempo,

a touch too fast. Dad's cine-camera never ran true
and we jerk unnaturally on the crab grass,
playing a game whose rules I have long since forgotten.

In half an hour we will run inside for a pitcher of lemonade.
In half an hour we will watch re-runs of *The Lone Ranger*.
In half an hour we will graduate, have our own children,

mortgage our own fine patches of crab grass.

II

There were four of us then: count us, four.
Before we collapsed from points on a square
to a fractured triangle with a central vacuum,

all things—cargo ships, B52s, spouses—sucked in
by the lack of you. Destroyed for not being you.
There's less of you recorded than the rest of us

as if you are prescient, one foot already out of the door,
when truth was you were always that bit different,
heading your own way. Your absence could be explained:

you were with your friend Shawn, setting light
to the neighbours' shed, or teaching earwigs to explode,
or eating raw eggs for quarters, or reading philosophy.

We three unlit where your shadow passes over.
Our ambitions stretched no further than jumping
off the garage roof without breaking our tibias.

Your heart lies beating on the grass. No-one sees it.
We are too busy out-dogging the dog, all-foured, or
itching our spines against gravel. Your heart

lies beating, persistent, between our impressions of
Foghorn Leghorn, our impressions of youthful indolence.
We were still immortal then. We had no inkling it could stop.

III

Our father the geologist. The materials scientist.
Our Grand Tour of the National Parks: Yosemite,
Umqua, Glacier, Lassen; places his family could

picnic while he filmed at the edges. He always
starts with us—perhaps to establish scale—
five-second vignettes before the gentle, persistent

pan to the right, his eye drawing him away
to more impressive and permanent features:
outcrops of eroded sedimentary layers, extinct

calderas. With a scientist's lust for taxonomy,
the signs are held steadily in shot: Lake Helen—
Elevation 6162; Snake River Road; Fountain

Paint Pots. But I fast-forward to the next snatch
of the next picnic; fascinated by the glimpses
of us, our clothes, our faces—unfashionable relics

of an era I can't believe we ever lived through.
Two sisters with neck-buttoned smock coats;
two brothers with mop-tops. We look like

the Kennedy children on the funeral newsreel.
Picture search past fumaroles, traffic-halting bears,
moose grazing peninsulas, sequoias, to the single

enduring close-up: three matching offspring
in cable-knits, riding the prow of a boat as it crosses
Jackson Lake. Nine counts: he raises the lens

and pulls focus back to infinity; to the Grand Tetons.
A gentle, persistent pan to the right. And then a sweep
of the sky, as though he expects a meteor shower.

IV

Because he is filming, there is none of him.
Because she is not, there is some of her.
She doesn't look at the lens. She doesn't smile,

except at us. They will separate soon
but at this point are simply pivoted
on a peak of grievances. And they are already

separated. Because he is filming, and she is in the film.
Mirroring the things she would later weep over:
that there was always some of her, and none of him.

V

Between Snake River and Jackson Hole, I was scanning
for the cavalry. In Jackson you could buy cowboy chaps
or Native American beads. There were life-sized carved chiefs

guarding the drugstore. Suddenly I could see John Wayne
on every corner and over the rim of a milkshake
in the Jackson Hole Hotel I peered through the drift

of station-wagons, aching for sight of some tumbleweed.
This barren stop that half the year is dry as Red-eye
leaving the palate and the other half is the province

of snow-chains and skiers had a clarity that nowhere
repeated. Those wide strident Wyoming roads that
led us away; you'd go eight hours without seeing

another car. Roads so blindingly straight they could
fool you into imagining corners; you'd drift
off the bitumen and plough through the cacti.

No-one would find the wreck for a week. Above the plains,
mountains loomed in the moonlight, counting out their high
lakes; the water retained somehow, almost unbearable.

VI

Rattling back west to our rented base
in a '64 Chevy, singing. Against the heat,
the eucalyptus scent, the aridity; the fluid

harmony of *Green Grow the Rushes O*.
Dad turning the fan up to full, the windows gaping,
Mum wafting herself with folded maps we had

driven off and the dust furring our tongues as we sang:
one is one and all alone and ever more shall be so.
Dad stopped not far from the Bay and fixed the radio.

VII

Stripping on Christmas Day. We played
in the buff; heavenly, seasonless California. Mum insisted
on doing a full roast dinner but after two mouthfuls

we ran outside to turn the sprinklers on. We baked
and browned through August, March, November.
Even the most deciduous trees were evergreen.

But that changeless state carries its changes
beneath the crust, and the smallest tremors would find us
rigid under the lintels. At kindergarten, we did quake drills.

We sensed that what seemed always a seamless same
had stored its surprises. For the most part we tried
to forget, live in shorts and sneakers, take advantage

of the heat. But under countless games
of Little League, under our lazy backs or bare feet,
a thousand lost seasons were reaching critical mass.

VIII

We learnt to swim in Strawberry Canyon pool.
Mum favoured the throwing-in method;
doggie paddle as a blind counterpoint

to drowning. We were all of us out of our depth.
My sister does a width entirely submerged,
only her buttocks breaking the surface;

she has to do the width to get the breath.
It was like that the whole way through—breathless,
hilarious, desperate. Our mother learned to dive

that summer, bracing her flimsy heart
with definitions of courage. Beneath her enthusiasm,
the certainty that it was all ending.

And beneath our swimming, our drowning.
And beneath our life, your death. The chill,
the watery suspension of gravity, the depth—

all carried in the glimmer of eight millimetres.
It is all so known to us now. The way a shadow
is distorted on the bottom of a pool, transformed

by the refractive index of water, and by our wakes.

Green

Looking down the long freeze of lawn,
grass creaking beneath your boots,
you know you have done wrong.
It should be beautiful:

the pond's veiled eye, the mist
of cobwebs there, and there.
The clutter of beehives
like a clapboard village beneath the trees.

You see only green,
the neighbourhood bully,
stripping off your white paint.
Green, which loiters invisible

in the breadbin to mug your loaves.
A strong smell of rot.
The pond never clears.
Alders strain to see themselves

like teenage girls at too small a mirror.
Yesterday, you could have pulled them out
with gloves. Now you'd need chainsaws,
pulleys, men with stubble and blasphemy.

Fish

On the third day, the sea spat out its fish.
Fish rained on the boats at their moorings,
netted themselves in the awnings of market stalls,
leapt athletically over the harbour wall.

They slid over roofs, dropped
into silent yards, spattered
on windowsills and paths,
their silver gleaming briefly blue.

Perfectly circular eyes
said nothing; said it wide.
Gills fluttered like the pages
of a magazine left on a café table.

They left themselves on café tables,
in doorways, in the clean linen
folded in its basket beneath a line.
And still more came.

By midday, the quayside fried with them.
A boil of scales: the small applause
they made for themselves at their effort
of finally breathing the whole sky.

Well

What I remember most was the white intensity
of your scream. We still tickled then, not too old
at seventeen. Your hair waved shamelessly;
elemental energy seeped through your skin as though
through fissures in a cooling mantle. You were
beyond belief, and words flooded my mouth
like grief as the drowning current of your laughter
swept me away. All this time I've missed you.

He works hard, you sigh, shaking your straight hair still.
Before your first child arrived, he'd capped the spring
and watched it dry. Marshy ground, he says, and a shrill
or social mother, are three of the most insidious things.
It's a family business now, he markets the water
while you man the phone and take orders. Your daughters'
chalky faces on the label make it sell and seem
like a litre of your purity for one pound nineteen.

You were my idol. On a field trip to Bradwell
all our kids ago, we catalogued crabs and seaweed
from the nuclear-heated streams that fed the beach.
We wrestled in the rancid estuary mud: strange
fish mutated from mermaids hewn out of women.
Our laughter shrieked curlews and oystercatchers
into the arms of Essex sky. Then, you were stronger
than even the tide flooding the scars of our footsteps.

Potato-printed crabs and starfish cover your kitchen,
limpet the fridge. Your elastic daughters are threading
shells of iridescent plastic into necklaces, itching
their eczema absently. Over the sink, a formal wedding
photograph parades you as you used to be. Leave him,
I want to say, as you flake your scalp and briefly scold
your desiccated children. Be wild, be fatal, be cold,
wash him away, I pray, under the hush of your breathing.

Pronoun

You never say her name; I never ask.
Pronouns walk us far

through the late night confessions,
next morning reassessments.

Her unsaid name blows about us
uncatchable as willowherb fluff

and as light
and as ready to seed;

and as sleeplessness
mottles the pigments

in my skin
her name spells itself in melanin:

a soft, emergent tattoo.
Once, before I started loving you,

I rang you at home.
A female voice on the answerphone

paired up your names like Jacks,
like silver cruets,

like evening gloves,
smoothing them out at the elbows.

Hers was there, pressed against yours,
and I thought of two corpses

discovered embracing
in the ruins of a fallen building,

having loved each other
to death.

Soup

Here, the sea is milk. A fishy milk, a cold
bouillabaisse of chalk and fin, served on a clatter
of stone. Within its clouded vision, cod fatten,
mackerel cut their zig-zags through the fog
like children dawdling to a school that has disappeared
and may not, they pray, be there when the whiteness clears.

These cliffs are temporary. Reduced and solid,
born from the warm, tropical broth of stock
and stored in a stack above, an Oxo block
now broken off in chunks and re-dissolved
in the cooler, less forgiving froth
of this liquid finger from the north.

So life revolves. We, too, are soup.
Temporarily solid vats of DNA
fleshed out just long enough to find a mate
with whom to create a different brew.
We dawdle through the fog. Circling above:
vagrants and migrants, the murderous cries of gulls.

Who Forgets

first of all, the right words.
And then, the day of the week, the names of friends.
He waits for them to fall from the sky, like birds.
The sky is very empty, blue.

His college years unravel like a scarf.
His marriage, taken piece by piece apart,
has detail scattered somewhere behind his right eye.
All that is left is sky.

If he was unfaithful, he forgets that too.
Not just the girl, her name, her face,
but all their love is a vapour trail.
The sky burns it back to blue.

These days are pure. Whatever pours in
pours out in the same measure.
Will not be stored.
Will pass, like weather.

He'd Push My Hands Together

to make me pray. His big hands; he had so much power
in his fingers and he'd squeeze like he could fuse the nubs
of my knuckles together if only God would give him
that extra p.s.i. The tendons rolled over each other

like garden canes in a gale and he wouldn't stop
until they crackled like the fireworks I could only ever
watch each year from my bedroom window. He said
Bonfire Night was heathen, like chocolate eggs,

carved pumpkins, Christmas trees; wouldn't have
such things in the house, and when he caught me
praying to the Easter bunny, he beat the skin off my thighs
with a four by two, and that's when I stopped praying.

God's love, he said, is a father's love, and both
he and God had to be harsh. Sometimes I couldn't
tell them apart. God the Father glared down invisibly
from the bathroom ceiling when I jerked myself off.

Father God glared at my unclasped hands from the pulpit
at Family Service and Evensong and I knew there'd be
hell to pay. At home, the comfort of instant retribution:
saying (or not saying) grace formed the holy trinity

of beatings: breakfast, lunch and tea. Morning prayer,
bedtime prayer, and at other times he'd vindictively
drop to his knees for no reason; I'd be doing my homework
or watching a wildlife documentary and he'd growl

Let us pray. But I was growing up and he was shrinking,
and my hands became his hands, and his diminished
until he hadn't the strength to fuse mine in supplication.
He called me from his bed and I made him wait, and wait,

almost drunk on the power. When he stopped calling
I went to him, his eyes glowing like the fragile bulbs
on a Christmas tree. *Pray for me*, he whispered,
and tapped his tiny hands against my palms.

Appointment

He fingers the ends with the care of a vet
handling a new-fledged baby bird.
'How would you like it cut?' he asks.
'Well,' I reply. 'I have a wedding to stop.'

I know I won't go. Just impediments
are for the movies. But I let him snip
through the blade of afternoon light,
layering out the splits, the kinks, the fluff
as thoughtfully as though I had the guts
to shout your name and race you to the bus.

Waiting for Scott

Scott waved *cheerio*. Someone else's father,
another Dad, grew whiter as we slept.
Through breakfast, I stood and watched the driveway,
kissing the window on my breath to make a Santa.

I scraped to school and thumped a shout
against the snow-closed cars.
Why won't his footprints show? The snow
and Mum have emptied all the cupboards.

At school, they're cutting card.
Christmas lanterns from my father's frozen skin.
Write a poem, they say, write a poem about snow.
Snow, I wrote, is God's eraser.

He draws me on to nothing; just the wind.
Straining for sense of his soft-hand voice,
his scent of earth and aftershave. Somewhere, here,
his careless nails shine black as pizza olives.

His name is melting. I call and spill its milk
below the sky. Pack ice flees, groans, drowns;
mutated into waves. So it was never land
and always water: listen. The thaw, talking.

Surfers at Sennen

They strip in the car park, always half-bare, dipping
into the open boots of hatchbacks, roofracks stacked
with plastic. As I leave the beach café with a fist
of Cornish cornets for the kids, one of them is leaning

against the whitewash; tanned, trousers at his ankles.
He stays like that for fifteen minutes, eyes on the breakers
while I mop ice-cream and wafer from clumsy mouths,
lick a drip of liquid from my forearm. The sea disgorges

dozens of them with each beat, and they rise up,
phantoms of my adolescence, riding my oestrogen.
I want to unzip them from their seal-skins, peel them
like bananas. Pull the rubber from their buttocks,

stuff my mouth with collagen. They don't look at me.
Their radios hum the long-range forecast. While I'm
packing the windbreak and half-chewed sandwiches
they'll be moving on to Porthcurno, Redruth, Newlyn.

Embassy Court

Embassy Court, on Brighton seafront, was designed by Wells Coates in 1935. Once popular with celebrities—and home to Rex Harrison and Keith Waterhouse, among others—it fell into disrepair in the 1970s. For many years, it stood dilapidated.

First Thought

She will be white. She will be tall, and white,
and so unthought as to stall the sea mid-wave.
Her curves, like touch. As though she'd stroked your face
just by your looking. And she will command light,
bend it, bow it, inspire and exhale it bright
as a first thought. And yours will fall away
to be replaced by nothing but clear, sheer, space.
Like creation itself. Like air. Like appetite.

And there—in the gap—all things are possible.
Undo, erase, and see what grows instead.
Unlearn your learning down to the last wrong
sum. To the last lost love. Give her your skull
and blast the present away. From emptiness,
a breath to build upon. From silence, song.

Little Miss Bauhaus

There's something about her purity appals.
Perfection is a dirty word when the dream
for pure white space that brought her into being
puts its foot down across the channel, falls
on necks and groins. At four, she's suspect. Think.
She stinks of German soap. She wasn't late.
She dominates with charm, and if you blink
she accidentally spells 'obliterate'.

Her skin is far too white against the grey
of Londoners in their tweed, and felt, and shame,
the burnt-out, bought-out Eden of the shops.
So if she mumbles anything, she prays.
That no-one traces back her father's name.
That she'll be standing when the whistling stops.

The Babe

The Sixties fizzing, aspirin in a glass.
Headache town, and she's a fist of it,
slammed against the temple of the bar,
the club, the Sunday lunchtime list of what
you'll never do again. The day's a blur.
She's the babe, and they're in love with her.
There isn't a soul worth knowing who hasn't slept
in her, and stirred, and stumbled out half-wrecked.

But they never stay. Their homes are somewhere else.
She's thinking of bottling up that small-hour smell
'cause that's the only thing to hang around.
That and her headache. Listen: the dim pound
of promises. Bastards. And always in her face:
the moon sliced up in the sea, keen as a blade.

What Happens to Women

It's what happens to women, no matter who you are.
Divine inside? They'll only see the face.
It's coming, despite your warmth, your grit, your heart—
the sudden shift from beauty to disgrace.
A light snapped off, and you're gone. You're in the dark.
No-one can see you now. You are unglued,
for while you slept, the world took you softly apart.
Now man after man walks through the ghost of you.

On a morning like any other, she wakes to find
her lover moved out, and all her admirers gone
from her steps, as if with one breath, one mind,
they abandoned their roses there like skeletons.
A half-penned love note stutters towards the sea,
embarrassed, undoing its 'love', and 'dear', and 'we'.

Refugees

On quiet afternoons, she's Africa.
Boundaries, borders lost in a soup of tongues,
and doors propped laughter wide, bright washing strung
between the balconies like celebration.
Women crouch over cooking pots on the stairs,
undressing yams with hands that know the task—
practical matriarchs that helm the ark,
their children alive and all in the one bed.

It's love, of sorts. And if some call her slut,
then damn those souls whose worship didn't last,
so only the piss-poor dispossessed see past
her windows glazed or unglazed or boarded up
like so many teeth just hanging on, or gone,
or filled haphazardly with something wrong.

Sunk

Beneath fathoms of air, the pressure is immense.
On deck, a peculiar light, severe and bleached.
Windows, if opened, explode onto the street,
bright with despair. No pitch, no present tense
will make this liner anything but sunk.
A current of urine snakes between the floors.
Funnels thicken, downpipes rust in chunks.
Doors gape. Brass numbers green in listless halls.

So many myths—the truth of the third age
is your fires stoked out, your name crossed off the page
in a single stroke. There, in the distance, singing—
a drift of something both commonplace and strange.
A slate of rain, the barometer stuck at Change.
The lifeboat cradles bare, their hooks still swinging.

Goddess

She will be white. She will be tall, and white.
For any woman can learn forgetfulness,
step from her past as from a small black dress,
become a thing you barely recognise.
No longer the passive victim of your slurs,
the wall for your tag, the vessel for your phlegm,
the fucked-up name you kick from friend to friend,
the shorthand code for ugliness like hers.

She will be Goddess. Fall to your knees and pray
that grace forgets; that memory isn't stored
in every cell beneath that concrete skin.
Once again, she will take your breath away,
she will be fought for, idolised, adored.
And you'll be lucky if she lets you in.

Fecundity

Birds thread themselves in flight
through telegraph wires that loop from house to house,
stringing all human life onto one thread
like the juicy necklaces of fish eggs
in farmyard ponds.

Fur, scent, a blast of flesh from the banks
of blackberry bushes, and the sense of life abundant,
life loosing itself, even underfoot,
snuffling blind and soft-nosed through the roots.

Outside the village hall
women gather together like nettle beds,
tall, proud, and fertile,
nodding the discrete white flowers
of their heads, concealing
the stinging barbs of their fine hairs.

Through closeted lanes,
sycamores pendulous with keys
that might unlock the heat like a jailer;
pregnant cumulus hovering like zeppelins
and the whole fat summer
threatening to drop, bloodless, to the ground.

BN1

Your place of birth?
An upstairs room
just after lunchtime.
September. Sunlight
turns the floor to honey.

> In Norfolk Square,
> luminous police
> harangue the drunks.
> White Lightning and Special Brew
> toast your arrival
> in their neighbourhood.

You are roared
through the last half foot;
sworn, slippery,
into your father's hands

> and a man who shouts
> at his invisible wife
> heaves the caterpillar skin
> of his sleeping bag
> over his shoulder.

You are beautiful.
Your skin is soaked
in air, your lungs crackle
open, you breathe

> while the girl at the till
> wears her boyfriend's
> jealousy. She counts out
> change. No-one even
> asks her to tell the lie.

You don't cry.
You blink at the light
as if you had no idea
there was an outside.
But this isn't half of it.

Through the glass,
up the street, people
once as new as you
are ticking like grenades
with their pins pulled,
none of them aware

you are sharing
the same thin air;
how we loved you
out of nothing.

Helping the Police with Their Enquiries

Three miles away, I feel the letter hit the mat.
It's been this way since I grew up.
For years I fought my senses,
tried not to see the monsters in the cup,

an accident lolling in milk, or in the sink
my father's cut whiskers and slub of foam
casually doodling the shape he would make
when his heart shut down. I almost don't go home,

as if turning tail could make the truth untrue.
The bus limps through the traffic and the rain,
mops up the loose pedestrians on the street,
as raindrops conspire into patterns, the same

dumb show. The way the girl's face
sprinkled itself on my windowsill,
made all of dust, and when I tried to rub her out
I ached like someone taken ill.

Over a week, she fell to me in scraps.
A daughter's name called empty in a park.
The egg-yellow insides of a shockless van.
The scent of rope and linseed in the dark.

It's all they've got to go on.
The van's ex-Telecom, they say.
I tell them I sense a wood, a railway line.
Her breath, marshmallow white, stopped yesterday.

Closer now, that letter's almost a shout. It's not a gift.
To taste, in my mouth, the envelope's cold blue,
to clench like the stiffened fist that held the pen
and scratched my name, to know it is from you.

The Gentle Way

Partner up. My first week
at the leisure centre's judo class,
and up steps you in a Persil-white
judogi, belted blue.

I know you from school, the hard nut
that smokes in the corner, says *fuck*
to the teachers; the boys are scared
of you. You gave Dean Moffat stitches.

Here, you're Diana—the instructor makes
your name all honey-sticky in his mouth.
But you are Di, Di-before-she-kills-you,
and you've been coming since you were ten.

You be the uke, you say in the side of your mouth
and knock me to the floor to help me deduce
the *uke* is the person being thrown. You demonstrate
your arm bars and joint-locking techniques

and make me whisper *thank you.*
The principle of You and I Shining Together
is slyly transformed into
You Finding New Positions For My Elbow.

Your Foot Wheels are sound, but you must practice
your Floating Hip, your Mountain Storm
and your Major Inner Reaping. All
are nearing perfection as I slide into the black.

Missing the Opera with My Sister

Rain is speaking now; we've had our turn
and found our mouths stuffed up like sawdust dolls.
Outside, the ground applauds. We never learnt
to dissolve our differences in alcohol.

Let's end this interval and pay the bill
before some arsehole stops to chat us up;
before we cry—as though we are infants still,
fighting for scrag-ends of our parents' love.

That lost love pours down through the years
like an army of driver ants picking clean
the bones of any child who's left to sleep.
As we were, by our parents' disbelief
that a child is capable of feeling pain
any more than, hitting the road, does rain.

Airtight

This was her breakfast this morning: coffee, toast
with thin-shred marmalade—lime—but just two bites
before scraping it into the bin. Later I'll touch
the craters her fingers left, the compressed crust
cut out by the mouth I'd die for. I'll memorise
the ragged half-moon of incisors that twist and jut

a little out of line. And then see if
that long-haired creep she kisses on the step
has had her yet. She must know he's not right
for her. A cheapening lout who makes me sift
through onion skins for evidence of his inept
attempts at 'love': the flabby Fetherlite.

There's nothing yet, thank God. But women are
a danger to themselves. She chats to guys
in Waitrose stacking shelves. Has no idea
the risks she takes each day: she's getting far
too friendly with the postman. That lamb-like smile.
But I'll protect her somehow. Keep her clear.

She's beginning to wreck my life. Even asleep
she ghosts her waking form across my screen:
rewind, replay and pause. Eating alone
or tripping across the lawn to hang out sheets
and smalls: the intimate loop of her routine
possesses me. She's thin now. White as bone.

She slept in her clothes last night. She's becoming a slut.
I've seen her weeping for hours into the phone
as though all that contrition could make her good
again. She's scared. She nailed her windows shut.
When the light goes off I'll call to let her know
I'm taking care of her. Well someone should.

Old School Friends

Suddenly they gleed into her life
clutching an insincerity of wishes,
condolence bundled up in bow and cellophane;
the sympathetic gabardine of every raincoat
puddling late November through her hall.

Like prows and bows and bells they came,
clanging their metalled hides against a grief
that had dropped out from the pockets of the sky,
a shot swan, an arrow of eye that had seen beyond
the glittering flattened fields of their insides.

There was an arrogance of time between them,
cushioned decades that they plumped and throned,
although for months before she'd sat alone,
blistering her throat with mute replies
as cancer slid its news beneath her door.

And then, one by one, they fetched their coats.
They made her up, and made themselves believe
their promises to write, or call. And took their keys.
And left their flowers to die before her eyes
as though they hadn't thought of her at all.

I Filled the Bath with Coty L'Aimant

I wanted to smell sweet. Arthur was calling.
Sweet, sweet William. Not mine, you know.

'Nanny Jill,' he said. 'Where are you going, Nanny Jill?'
'The Palladium,' I said. The Palladium.

What a treat. Arthur was calling, see.
I had that Friday off. My birthday.

Twenty-three. I ran the hot water
first because it ran cold so quickly.

So quickly. Little William, sweet William.
'Goodbye, Nanny Jill,' he said, and I corrected him.

'Goodnight, William,' I said. 'It's good*night*.'
My sweetheart was calling for me,

I hadn't much time, had to iron
my dress. Blue it was, with daisies

and a white collar. Blue. Skin. Like—like—
Oh my little William. But he was all

tucked up see, all tucked up, I tucked him up
and filled the bath with Coty L'Aimant.

Ran the hot water first, went to iron—
my dress—blue with daisies, blue.

Skin, like—like curd.
One second, and you're in darkness.

No going back, can't have it back.
One second that could have been different.

My life is worth nothing:
that's what they think, these folk

that drop coins into my blanket.
Buy a life.

But I had a life.
I left it behind, is all.

In that second,
the one I couldn't get back to.

Because you can't go back.
And you can't close your eyes.

There's the screaming, see.
The screaming. I knew, I knew, I knew—

too late. Just a second, William.
Just a second.

Darkness.
Blue.

Skin.
He'd had his bath. I don't know why.

I don't know why he did it.
His skin was all there.

In the bath. Not on him.
Little thing. Sloughed off

like, like curd.
That smell.

Coty L'Aimant.
The heat.

I wanted to smell sweet.
Sweet William.

It ran cold so quickly.
Arthur was calling, see.

The Palladium. Blue daisies.
'Goodbye Nanny Jill,' he had said to me.

And I corrected him.
I corrected him.

One Way of Falling

September in the park. The stacks of chairs
outside the council-run café lean, sway
like sextons over some undug plot. Two pairs

of speakers wring out love songs; wet the heads
of awkward knock-kneed girls on rollerblades,
au pairs half-minding other people's kids.

Their forearms pucker gooseflesh to the sun,
buckle for one last kiss that may or may
not be the constipated not-quite-done

of summer's thrust. Behind the violins,
the second-class arrangements of the day,
do those that have their minds on other things—

that clap politely on the bowling green,
that call to dogs to 'leave' and 'come'—do *they*
detect the hush of groundsmen moving in?

The elms undress. Though once quite overwrought
for springs that gouged their trunks with him plus her,
as lichen scabs the lovers' sums to nought

they strip beyond the bounds of taste, to bone.
Yes, have it all. There's nothing left to say
that wouldn't be better said out loud, alone.

How Things Are on Thursday

How Things Are on Thursday

Daddy is lying on the floor
you tell the telephone.
You take a message, like a secretary

in handwriting that is extra neat,
and felt-tip a heart around your name
before sliding it under

Daddy's nose. The beer can
is his baby, crooked in his arm.
He sings it lullabies.

You put yourself back under the curtain
and watch for nobody coming.
If nobody comes

you will stay a shape under the cloth
like a sheeted sofa in a creaky house
where someone should have an adventure.

The window gives you its cold. You breathe
on it, little rivers. The house sits
at the top of the hill like an open eye.

It has been dark for ages now.
Below, the pubs belch out the drunks
whose laughter makes you want to cry.

Why Sleep is Dangerous

In the centre of their bed is a current
of icy water. It has come all the way
from the Arctic, shed from a glacier.
You mustn't swim there. You mustn't
make the mistake of crawling into it,
you will be frozen and swept away.

In the centre of their bed is a forest.
Ever since you were born it has been
impenetrable. They cannot cross it.
It is so overgrown that the brambles
have choked themselves, and all
the oxygen has gone, pushed out by thorns.

In the centre of their bed is a nest
of snakes, two kinds, the kind that squeeze
and the kind that bite. The venom makes you
talk gibberish, then swells your tongue
into a small planet. You cannot live there,
poisoned and hugged into silence.

In the centre of their bed is a wound.
Even when they don't try to pick it
it doesn't heal, just seeps and bleeds.
It may be infected. You mustn't mention it.
If it hears itself being talked about, it will
leap up with a roar and swallow you.

In the centre of their bed is a word
that nobody knows. It opens castles.
It undoes curses, and men that were turned
into beasts turn back into men when
you say it. But you cannot say it.
It has no sound; it barely dreams of being.

Where to Go

At lunch the year ten girls
are comparing heels.
Boyfriends' names
shiver in the air like
breath on the sports field.

You spent two lessons in the loos.
Now, a knot of girls around the sink
try on each other's lippies—
Rum Spice, Chilli Passion.
Your Mum's got cancer.

Debbie wants to know how to
French kiss. Shara demonstrates,
finger and thumb making lips,
tongue poking shrieks of disgust
from its audience.

The smell of Superkings
and hairspray. Someone needs
change for the Tampax machine.
Bella's getting highlights.
Your Mum's got cancer.

When She Pretends to Be Swimming

They uncover her, week after week.
Your occupation? Roll up your sleeve.
Any history of this in the family?

Drop the shoulder. There's the girl.
An awkward squeeze. The doctor's young.
His hands tremble as he tries to feel

the size and shape of what is wrong.
There's the girl.
Her left breast

sat out in the air like it's on holiday.
Though she's never gone topless.
Dropped the straps, maybe.

The doctor's hands move tenderly.
Her husband used to
operate her like machinery.

She made him stop. It's been so long
since she was touched. He said
I wish you weren't so complicated.

These days, she comes with notes.
After the hospital gown, the nudity,
they uncover her further.

Her breast stripped off
down to the sternum.
Then, drugs

that uncover her scalp.
There's the girl.
Under the wig.

Walls the colour of biscuits only half done.
Half-baked ideas like poisoning her
to make her well.

But that's alright.
She will be sick. She will lie back
and let others make a better job of it.

What Gives

You take the bus alone. Climb up top,
sit at the front to be sure you can see
everything. The city lurches. You watch

the driver through the angled mirror
made for vandals. He threads the wheel
through his hands, quarter by quarter.

You wouldn't like to steer a bus.
It doesn't feel safe turning corners,
it leans. Though you know that's just

a feeling. The High Street's choked
with shoppers, other people's daughters
gaggled and giggling, throwing back Coke

at the edge of the precinct. Push-chair jams;
elephant women burdened with kids, and too
many bags, and not enough hands.

Elderly men not quite sure where to go.
And boys you recognise from school
trying to push each other into the road.

Your bus swings out, barely missing
the number five. A different top deck:
two leather-jackets, kissing.

The city's surviving department store says twelve.
A man does up his daughter's coat. You left
your father nursing a Resolve,

your homework done, the dog in its basket, fed,
your mum in bed, the punctuation
of tidy piles of clothing on the stairs.

You went to the library. You know you shouldn't't've.
Got on the internet, Googled her operation.
'Removing the Mass', it said, and lots of stuff

about catching it early, which she didn't.
You printed it, then threw it in the bin.
Certain information is forbidden.

Because as long as no-one says it, it isn't true.
Like pubic lice, like HIV, like the thing
where Hitler murdered all those Jews.

You sit on the words like Miss Priest
makes you sit on your hands.
You don't like to think about it.

Your parents don't want you to.
You all laugh at the sitcoms.
But it's still there. It's like the goo

under your BCG scab, only bigger.
At least no-one can see it
when you're swimming.

The terminal stop. Middle of nowhere.
The engine dies; the driver goes outside, his cigarette
smoking holes into the pause before new fares.

If the bus would keep going.
If you could just stay there.
You'd feel better, not knowing.

Who Marks Himself

He has taken to running. It's easy,
one foot in front of the other, and quiet,
nothing but the steady rhythm

of his trainers thumping the pavement,
his breath falling into step between the footfalls
in and out and in and out and in and out and

in those first few yards from the gate,
the distance between him and home
doubling and doubling again,

he feels like sprinting.
The words that crowd his head in the house
string out like beads on a necklace,

further and further apart,
and by the time he reaches
the turn onto the towpath

there's nothing
but the thread those words were on,
the silences between them strung out

into one long empty road
that twitches to the beat
of his footfalls

like a stave marked out
with bars of four-four time,
waiting for a new tune.

The Dancer

She could fold herself in a perfect half
like a dollar bill in a waitress's apron pocket,
waiting to be spent.

She could fold herself like an envelope,
the flat white surface of her thigh against
the flat white surface of her breastbone,
you could lick the edges of her together,
your saliva gumming her closed.

She could fold herself as flour
is folded into beaten eggwhite,
without knocking out the air.

And you would fold her back on herself
like the sleeve of an ironed shirt,
press her knee gently against her shoulder
before you entered—I know
this alien intimacy because once

you pressed my knee gently against my shoulder
before you entered, forgetting
that not all women are dancers.

Now you have returned to her suppleness
I am learning to fold in my own way—
like a bad hand in five-card brag,
concealing my face, rubbing
the over-stretched elastic of my ligaments.